An Introverted, Wanderlusting Martial Artist's Commentaries on MUSASHI'S DOKKŌDŌ

Gregor Fjellrev

BLUE FORGE PRESS
Port Orchard, Washington

An Introverted, Wanderlusting Martial Artist's
Commentaries on Musashi's Dokkōdō
Copyright 2022
by Gregor Fjellrev

First Print Edition June 13, 2023

ISBN 978-1-59092-893-6

Parchment page image by kjpargeter on Freepik
Leather cover image by Freepik

All rights reserved including the right to reproduce this book or portions thereof except in the case of short excerpts in reviews of the book. For information about subsidiary rights, write to: blueforgegroup@gmail.com

This is a work of fiction. Names, characters, locations, and all other story elements are the product of the author's imagination and are used fictitiously. Any resemblance to actual persons, living or dead, or other elements in real life, is purely coincidental.

Blue Forge Press is the print division of the volunteer-run, federal 501(c)3 nonprofit company, Blue Legacy, founded in 1989. Dedicated to empowering artisans marginalized due to race, age, ability, sexuality or economics, we have four divisions: Blue Forge Press, Blue Forge Films, Blue Forge Gaming, and Blue Forge Records. Find out more about us at www.MyBlueLegacy.org and www.BlueForgePress.com

Blue Forge Press
7419 Ebbert Drive Southeast
Port Orchard, Washington 98367
blueforgepress@gmail.com
360-550-2071 ph.txt

INTRODUCTION

God dag, dødligers. I would say I am known as Gregor Fjellrev, but I am not particularly known at time of writing, so I won't say that. Instead, I shall continue to be a generally incomprehensible ponderer of things, a social hermit of an actor, writer, musician, and carpenter who likes to train in martial arts within a secluded clearing in a local forest, to folk metal from various countries playing in the background. If you are somehow still curious after all of that madness and have not already resigned me as a gibbering fool, the folk metal types I make my training montages out of are Mongolian, Polish, Norwegian, and Slovak, with a healthy dash of Finnish Industrial Power Metal for good measure.

    I also possess the skills of pattern recognition, deductive reasoning, and critical thinking, as well as a general knowledge of history, which makes me more qualified as a general advisor than about ninety percent of consulting firms combined. I suppose being a student of strategy and tactics also helps, so good thing I'm one of those, too.

      As I write this, it's the morning after I fought math again, and my brain is still sore. We're calling it a draw. If you must know, I was trying to determine the orbital plane of Proxima Centauri B, but for some reason that number is lost. Apparently, an observatory in Australia burned down, and presumably it had that information. The other numbers we have on the system suggest that the orbital plane of the exoplanet should also be recorded, but mysteriously, this one measurement is absent. Were it not for the fact that the system is currently within the skies of the southern hemisphere and my funding is next to zero, I would grab a telescope, bike to where it can be seen, and just take the measurements myself. It should also be noted that while in the middle of writing the following commentaries, I suddenly discovered that the reference I was using was fundamentally different from the actual translation, as the wording was heavily simplified in order to make more broad sense for a Wikipedia article. I found this incomprehensible, as the translation I found and used as my primary reference all had the Principles in single sentences, which to me, warranted no such simplification. Perhaps this was some clever scheme to get someone so worked up over it, they would decide to make their own translation and commentaries. If that truly is the case, I tip my hat to you, schemer of the Wikipedia article. At least, I would, if I looked good in hats and possessed any. I do not, however. That all said...

      GODS DAMN IT THE NUMBERS CAN BE CALCULATED, I JUST REALIZED THIS SEVEN MONTHS LATER. Proxima Centauri B's Orbital Plane is 0.304 AU, and orbits at a speed of 54.81 kilometers per second, with a margin for error of approximately 0.35, considering the system's observed eccentricity.

An Introverted, Wanderlusting Martial Artist's Commentaries on Musashi's Dokkōdō

Gregor Fjellrev

FOREWORD

Miyamoto Musashi created the 21 Principles of *Dokkōdō*, *The Path I Go Alone*, a week before his death on the 13th of June, 1645, dedicating it to his favorite disciple, Terao Magonojō, himself a famed swordsman during the Edo period of Japanese history, to whom Musashi's *Book of Five Rings* was also dedicated. Both works were entrusted to Terao, who presumably burned the original *Book of Five Rings* on Musashi's orders, given that the complete original work cannot be found.

If this is indeed the case, and Terao did burn the original works, I would surmise that it was to prevent it from being such a sought-after artifact that men would tear each other to pieces over the right to possess, which Musashi may very well have (correctly, if I might add) anticipated. It is far from outside the realm of possibility, given that he was a master strategist and swordsman.

My will to create a translation of my own

stems from spiteful inspiration brought on by the painfully oversimplified Wikipedia article on the text, a lack of works I have been able to find regarding *Dokkōdō* and the desire to correct this, and the fact that I seem to share in several of Musashi's traits (wanderlust, a passion for martial arts and strategy, and heavy introversion.) However, one should also consider the Japanese language itself. It is a notoriously passive-aggressive language even/especially in 1645. The strongest insult one can say in Japanese nowadays is essentially 'bastard,' but the way it works is more akin to an English-speaker saying '*you*' with a tremendous side-eye. When you walk into a Japanese language class, you are essentially expected to apologize to the teacher for existing, whereas in Hebrew, 'bitch' translates directly and you're expected to insult the teacher back when they insult you for entering the room. Naturally, Musashi may have genuinely not had the words required to pen what would be considered his 'true' thoughts on the matter. Some people also might argue that Musashi had no 'true' thoughts on these matters, and that the widely-interpretable nature of the wording and language used is part of the point. It is also the case that some people are as pretentious as they are scared of opinions and of having them, and it is also the case that some interpretations of Sun Tzu's *Art of War* boil down to him saying 'if you're surrounded, try not to be surrounded because being surrounded is bad' and 'try setting people on fire in battle, as people generally don't like being set on fire,' which just sounds like common sense as far as strategy is concerned.

COMMENTARIES ON THE 21 PRINCIPLES

WAIT JUST A DAMNED MINUTE
I just found the original transcription on the internet, as well as a digitized transliteration of Terao's transcription of the Principles, and these are NOT the same words that the Wikipedia article had, fucking hell this changes everything, doesn't it? Shit, *several* of these are practically fundamentally different between the two. Gods damn it, I need to attempt my own translation now, I think. Hang on, I'm gonna go check out a Japanese dictionary from the library or something. Shit...

5/14/2022, 12:59 PM PST – *Approximately 40-50 minutes after my last entry*
I've managed to get down to a local pub near the library to eat some lunch before taking a crack at translating Dokkōdō myself, following my discovery

of the original digitized transcription, and a scholarly translation of it that renders the wordings of several, if not all of the 21 Principles fundamentally different than what is listed within Dokkōdō's Wikipedia entry, a clearly simplified version that I must suspect the author was in quite the hurry to write. You see, you can't just simplify the wording of a 17th century Japanese script and *not* expect that to fundamentally change the definitions and subsequent interpretations! You just *can't!* I've said before that it's one of the most subtle and passive-aggressive languages out there, and as such, warrants transcription on the most literal level possible before you can glean interpretations from it! I am very much grumbling in scholarly nature at this oversight that I would have personally easily pierced through and not made, and I am also very hungry so that may be only amplifying the sheer amplitude of my grumbles and gripes. Once I finish up here, my next course is to the library to use their WiFi to continue my work on making my commentaries actually worthwhile, given that the prior commentaries I have already made are based upon the Wikipedia entry for Dokkōdō. The original commentaries will remain on a separate document that will be hidden from publication, because it makes me look very silly. At least, more so than I presumably already look.

1:56 pm PST – *about 10-15 minutes after arriving at the Kistap Regional Library in Port Orchard, Washington*

    I've got some scrap paper, and images of the digitization of the text as well as the original text on my laptop screen, along with Teruo Machida's translation of Dokkōdō (entitled "The Last Words of Miyamoto Musashi: An attempt to translate his Dokkōdō"; Bulletin of Nippon Sport Science University, received Oct 31, 2011, Accepted Dec 23, 2011). All of my notes herein are based upon these three references, as well as this Japanese to English dictionary present at the library (Kodashana's Romanized Japanese-English Dictionary, ISBN 4-7700-1603-4)

    As much as this Japanese-English dictionary is almost 400 years removed, Sakoku only ended in 1853 and Musashi had in fact been alive for the first twelve years of the isolation era of Japan, so that may have affected his worldview, to be honest. By the gods, it must've been a triple combo of adopting Buddhism, being an old man, *and* the confiscation of all weapons and closing of the country (save for the one port city the Dutch were allowed to trade with.)

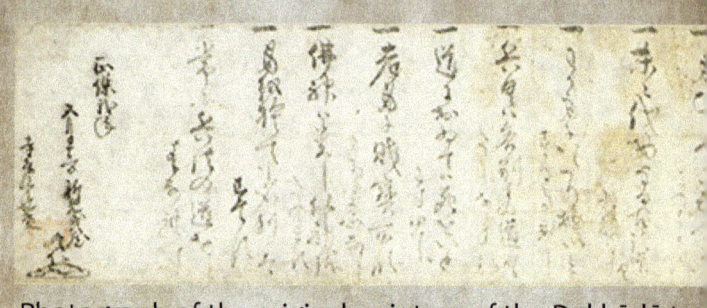

Photograph of the original scripture of the Dokkōdō text

一 身ひとつに美食をこのます
一 末々代物なる古き道具所持せす
一 わか身にいたり物いミする事なし
一 兵具ハ各別よの道具たしなます
一 道におゐてハ死をいとわす思ふ
一 老身に財寳所領もちゆる心なし
一 佛神ハ貴し佛神をたのます
一 身を捨ても名利はすてす
一 常に兵法の道をはなれす

（異筆）

正保貳年

五月十二日　新免武藏　玄信（花押）

寺尾孫之丞殿

A digitized instance of the text for the purpose of clarity

penned by Terao Magonojō.

獨行道
一 世々の道をそむく事なし
一 身にたのしみをたくます
一 よろつに依怙の心なし
一 身をあさく思世をふかく思ふ
一 一生の間よくしん思わす
一 我事におゐて後悔をせす
一 善悪に他をねたむ心なし
一 いつれの道にもわかれをかなします
一 自他共にうらミかこつ心なし
一 れんほの道思ひよるこころなし
一 物毎にすきこのむ事なし
一 私宅におゐてのそむ心なし

what is written.

(1.) *Hitotsu: Yoyo no Michi o somuku Koto-nashi*

Hitotsu is the word for the horizontal line indicating a new prose or phrase, akin to if someone were to verbally declare "New line" or "New thought." The word *Yó*, translates as "The world," or "Society," with "*Yóyo*" indicating a plural. However, given that the plural form of *Yó* does not indicate multiple worlds, bur rather additional emphasis, this is less *worlds* and more *the World*, like one were to say "The whole Earth." The *no* itself indicates possession, like the English apostrophe-s ('s) does the same. Thus, *Yóyo no* would be translated as "The world's" or "Society's," with *Michi* meaning "Road" or "Path." *Somuko* means 'to disobey or deviate,' while *koto* means "Matters" or "Affairs," and *-nashi*, "Without." This particular introverted martial artist would argue that because there is no reference to the self within the line, Musashi likely would be acknowledging that the world (as in, the Earth and not the machinations of the Humans upon it) is a grand and mysterious entity whose motives, if existent, are incomprehensible. However, even before adopting Buddhism formally, Musashi seemed content with this, and to simply walk along whatever path presented itself. In this retrospect, one might interpret that Musashi was reflecting with quiet satisfaction that he had 'walked the world's path without dissent towards its ways.' With this being one of the 21 Principles that he followed in life, Musashi may very well have been mentioning this as the way he had gone about life, whilst recommending others to try that way of thinking on for size. Thus, I would interpret this line as follows: *(Walk) the World's Path without dissent to its Ways.*

      This is fundamentally different from what I had initially lifted directly from the Wikipedia article, as to 'accept everything just the way it is.' The World, let's be honest, refers to the planet of Earth and its natural workings, rather than its self-proclaimed dominant species. Musashi does not ask the reader to accept all things the way they are, he instead asks that one does not resist the will of 'mother earth,' as it were. This is once again, a far cry from 'accept everything just the way that it is,' and makes a hell of a lot more sense, if you ask me. We must also consider the contextual factors for Musashi's words. He essentially had a four-hit combo of being an elderly Japanese man and Ronin-turned-Buddhist who had just seen twelve years of Japan being completely isolated from the rest of the world. This would do a number on anyone, let's be honest. In his scholarly paper, Machida arrives at a very similar translation to my own, "I will not oppose the ways of the world."

(2.) *Hitotsu: Mi ni Tanoshimi o takuma-zu*

With *Mi* referring to the self, and *ni* being a noun-following particle denoting that the noun preceding it is 'at/on/in' *Mi ni* basically means "I will." *Tanoshimi* means 'pleasure,' whether physical or mental. Simply put, the concept of pleasure to some end. *Takuma-zu* is something I can't find in my library Japanese-English dictionary, but one must consider the context of the language indeed being a little under 400 years removed from the text I'm trying to translate, so I'm willing to defer to the explanation from Machida, *"'takuma-zu is comprised of the verb 'takumu' and the phrasal verb 'zu,' 'takumu' has the meaning of 'conceive, invent, plan, aspire' and 'zu' is a negative suffix, to negate a preceding verb with determination."*

By this logic, *takuma-zu* would mean 'to not plan.'

Machida's translation lists the second Principle as *"I will not seek pleasurable activities,"* which is a perfectly sensible and logical translation in and of itself. However, I find it difficult to believe that this is Musashi's intent with this line. True as it may be that as a Buddhist, he would highly value asceticism and the not seeking of physical pleasure, I believe there is a difference between seeking and planning. Musashi, being a martial artist and strategist, would understand well that plans never survive first contact with the enemy, and to *plan* pleasure would be even more folly. With the prior Principle encouraging one to not disagree with the way of the world, this suggests a more 'going with the flow' lifestyle being encouraged, rather than one of total renouncement. Remember that pleasure is not limited to sexual matters, like what many modern audiences would initially place their minds at when thinking of the term. In American English, to *pleasure* as a verb carries a slang denotation of bringing someone to orgasm. However, pleasure can also mean fulfillment or accomplishment, as accomplishing a goal or completing a project brings to many, large amounts of satisfaction and therefore pleasure.

I argue that Musashi, rather than encouraging people not to seek out pleasurable activities, instead encourages people to *not plan to be pleased*, so as to avoid disappointment should the plan deviate for any reason. It should be noted that he clearly does *not* mean "plan to be disappointed," merely that one should not hold an expectation of pleasure, thus:

I will not plan pleasure.

(3.) *Hitotsu: Yorozu ni Eko no Kokoro nashi*

The characters appear to be separate on both the original script and the digital transliteration, and on their own, we have yo, which in this context is about the equivalent of an exclamation point (!) and *ro* indicating an imperative, so we have two different kanji marking this Principle as 'extra important,' as it were. The *-zu* suffix nowadays is the *-tsu* suffix, but carries seemingly the same denotation, indicating further emphasis. Clearly, either Terao or Musashi himself thought this one was particularly important. *Ni*, once again, indicates that the prior noun is 'at/on/in.' In Machida's translation, *Yorozu* means 'everything,' and that makes sense to me, so I'll go with that. Thus, *Yorozu ni* would at a most literal translation, mean "Everything will." Machida also notes that several words are repeated in Chinese for stylistic reasons, and that would explain the Chinese characters in this Japanese text.

Kokoro is a word meaning "Mind" or "Mentality," a concept that Musashi heavily emphasized the honing and training of. *Nashi* once again indicating the absence of something, and I'm still not able to find *Eko* in this dictionary I'm using, though Machida's translation has it to mean "Bias," "Preference," or "Prejudice." with *no* following *Eko*, this tells me something along the overall lines of:

It is extra important to have not a mentality of prejudice.

The grains of salt to be taking with this, and basically everything else in these commentaries, is that I am not a Japanese-speaker, and my resources are limited. About the only traits I share in common with Musashi is a passion for martial arts and learning in general, being heavily introverted, and romanticizing of a solitary, nomadic lifestyle. Musashi understood the importance of both being stalwart and immovable, but always going with the flow and being able or willing to change and accept new truth. To this end, Musashi asks us to remain true to ourselves and how we wish to live and see the world, whilst also being able and willing to accept new knowledge should it present and prove itself. The difference between stalwartness and prejudice, in my opinion, is that one defends you from ignorance and other ruinous powers, while the other stops you from growth. Musashi understood this diad well, and asks us to be mindful of both sides of that coin, because both possess great moral value when implemented correctly. The challenge lies in the implementation itself, and is a constant one, that demands vigilance against chaotic infiltrators, and openness to positive change.

(4.) *Hitotsu: Mi o asaku omoi Yo o fukaku omou*

Mi, once again, the self. *O* marks the direct object of a clause, indicating that this particular Principle is something that the self should do. As much as I see the word *asaku*, formed within the digital transliteration as *a sa ku*, I can't figure this one out owing to my inexperience with the nuances of the Japanese language. *Asa* translates as 'morning,' with *ku* indicating a verb. So clearly, *asaku* is an adverb that I can't find a definition for. *Omoi yo* seems to indicate something along the lines of 'weight of the world,' but that may be a hell of a stretch, as *omoi* on its own seems to mean something being heavy or severe, but every instance of the kanji as it appears within the digitization appears to be within a context of remembrance or recollection, the phenomenon of memory. In the context of *omoi Yo o*, it would probably help if I actually could figure out a definition of *asaku*. Machida's translation has *asaku* as 'shallow' or 'unimportant,' likely in the context of 'insignificant,' while *fukaku* is to indicate its opposite (deep, massive, important.) Plugging the three kanji I see into my dictionary as best I can (*fu ka ku,*) I find the *ka* character to indicate a preceding clause as a question, while *fu* only appears once within my dictionary as the first part of *fuke*, 'dandruff.' I'm willing to chalk this one up to linguistic evolution and the difference almost 400 years makes, though it would be pretty hilarious if Musashi was asking if there was dandruff in his hair and Terao mistakenly penned that. By the gods, wouldn't that be the day if Musashi was actually muttering about how he found some morning dandruff in his hair and Terao, ever faithful, transcribed what he heard. Or perhaps he was being oddly poetic about it, saying something like 'I am as significant a weight to the world as the dandruff in my hair is to my head,' but I somewhat doubt it.

I am an insignificant weight upon the world so grand.

Machida's translation has this line as *"I consider myself unimportant, but not the world so great and deep."* Which is probably a better worded-out version of what's written on the original text, as well as a more clearly construed version of what I've arrived at. Musashi, being an elderly Japanese man who had just seen twelve years of *Sakoku* could have been easily undergoing a veritable whirlwind of emotions and crises of identity, and may have been thrown into a massive depressive state upon Japan's sudden and total isolation. Though I don't know whether or not Musashi ever traveled beyond Japan, it's entirely possible that any plans he may have had to were suddenly stripped away by the *Sakoku* taking place, which would make one feel entrapped in a cage. However large a cage the size of an entire island country may be, at the end of the day, a cage it remains. Japan had entered a sort of 'time-out corner' that Musashi would not be able to claim responsibility as among the reasons for, but feeling the effect of it still would make anyone feel like garbage. The line, however, could as easily be a rallying cry to the self as it would be a lament to what opportunity now seems fiction in the face of some other idiot deciding that because someone else was one way, now you have to suffer its consequences as well, though you did nothing wrong. I wonder what Musashi's opinions on *Sakoku* were. I find it easy to believe he dissented it. This hermitic, heavily introverted martial artist certainly would and does despise the idea of being so thoroughly deprived of the privilege of wandering. Even if the size of a nation, a cage is a cage all the same.

(5.) *Hitotsu: Isshô no Aida Yokushin omowa-zu*

Isshô means "throughout one's lifetime," or moreover "all throughout life." *Aida*, "time" in the context of its passage, i.e., "during this time." I'll get back to *omowa-zu* in a moment, but there is a single conjugation that exists, *omowazu*, which means 'unintentional.' *Yokushin* is said to mean "desire, greed, craving" in Machida's translation, but I find it hard to see, given that the Kanji used are not the ones for greed in particular. Once again, probably linguistic evolution at work. So be it. I personally find desire, greed, and craving to all be three different things, so in the interest of being an introverted martial artist with wanderlust unfulfilled, I'm leaning more towards *desire* on this one, the wishing to partake. Where I see greed as the wish to possess in excess, and craving being essentially desire squared, desire holds no moral sin, because otherwise that would be silly.

Plugging everything into itself and then trying to find a grammatically sensible wording, we arrive at several possibilities, all of which carry their own meaning depending on which specific words are used. Yeah, I know that's kinda how sentences work, but bear with me. We can find ourselves with the following:

Throughout life's passage, do not be dictated by desire/Greed.

It seems like common sense, encouraging one to not succumb to excess of want that turns into greed or jealousy, carrying more of a 'know thyself' connotation as well. Machida's translation has it as *"I will be free of desire throughout my entire life,"* and while that makes sense in a very Buddhist context, not to mention Musashi being a week from death at the time and very possibly trying to speedrun the path to enlightenment, considering that Musashi also encouraged not regretting one's actions, I find those two concepts mutually exclusive, while the simple encouragement to not be a greedy prick to be mutually inclusive with not bearing regrets.

(6.) *Hitotsu: Waga-Koto nioite Kôkai o se-zu*

I can't tell if I'm an idiot or my dictionary is incomplete, because I can't find *waga* as a possessive pronoun as Machida's translation has it. The only context I see is in the word *wagamáma*, or 'selfishness,' and it looks nowhere near to the Kanji on the digital transliteration. I'll file that one under linguistic evolution again, and go along with Machida's translation that *Waga-Koto* basically means 'my matters/my things.' *nioite* appears to be the conjugation of *ni oi te*, but the only context I can find for the Kanji used for *oi* is in the sort of 'hey!' one yells to get someone's attention. *Te* is the name of the Okinawan predecessor to Karate, whose closest modern counterpart is the Karate style of Shuri-te, but I doubt this is what that means. Once again, linguistic evolution continues to be the bane of my existence. As a conjugation, it is said to reference the previous word. *Kôkai* directly translates as 'regret,' so I'm glad I've finally got something easy to translate. *Se-zu* as it's written looks like a conjugation of *suru-zu*, *suru* meaning 'to engage in,' in this context likely meaning what one has done, or their deeds in life. *Zu* once again is a negative denotation, saying 'not,' typically in the context of 'don't,' indicating that one should not engage in *Kôkai*, regret.

My matters are deeds without regret.

I would argue that Musashi is in this context, affirming a lack of regrets for his deeds and accomplishments in life, a worthy thing to do, renouncing regret. Being in the last section of his mortal life, Musashi's Buddhist adaptations would very much encourage him not to regret what he had done in life as he reflected on it, as regret is very commonly considered a prison that bars progress from occurring, in whatever form that may be. Musashi held himself to a very strict moral code in life, and adherence to that code would be what assured that he could not be blamed for whatever he had done, from his acquisition and use of his martial skill, as well as his creation of the Book of Five Rings. With *Sakoku* having been active for the last twelve or so years of his life, Musashi may very well have entered a deep state of regret-born depression as he would have wondered if he was partly responsible for Japan's forced isolation from the world, and being put in a proverbial time out-corner for all the infighting and violence that was occurring up until then. However, Musashi being one man, though a very skilled and strategically brilliant man, cannot and should not take responsibility for the entire state of his homeland. Though his knowledge and skill could and arguably would advance how fighting was fought, it is how that knowledge is implemented that decides one's path. Musashi cannot be blamed for opening the door, as it were, only those who walk through it are responsible for their fate and the fate of those around them as a consequence of walking that path.

If Musashi was as wise and smart as they say, then he would not have regrets for his deeds, as is clear in this line, that he had at the very least come to terms with his lifetime before its end. Yes, very Buddhist indeed. Seems he went all in on it, if taking upon a Dharma name wasn't already a hint enough of that fact.

(7.) *Hitotsu: Zen-Aku ni Ta o netamu Kokoro nashi*

Zén'aku translates directly as "Good and evil" (though the dictionary I'm using actually has a typo at this page and says 'go and evil,' but these things happen.) *Ta* means 'other' or 'another,' and *netamu* means to become jealous or envious. *Kokoro nashi* appears here again, carrying the context of 'the mind should be absent of (subject), in this case *netamu*, jealousy.'

Good and/or evil, jealousy should be absent from the mind.

I personally define jealousy and envy as two separate things, where *envy* is when you covet something you do not possess and someone else does, while *jealousy* is when you actively want to take that which you covet from someone else who possesses it. To this end, jealousy does not require the absence of a coveted item from the possession of the jealous individual. Jealousy can take the form of a desire to hoard that which is coveted, and to keep it away from all others. Indeed, that should be absent from the mind. Stellar findings, Musashi.

I find myself contemplating a more cynical elderly Musashi, fully aware of how ridiculously simple most 'old man wisdom' is at its core, and just going with it, saying something astoundingly obvious whenever some young and aspiring warrior-scholar approached and asked for wisdom. It could've been something along the lines of "O, great Musashi, what is your wisdom?" and then Musashi responds "Don't be a dick" and then the aspirant enthusiastically goes "By the gods, that's genius! That's a good wisdom!" and then goes off and has an epiphany while Musashi just rolls his eyes.

My YouTube recommended feed manages somehow to simultaneously laser-focus on how best to try to feed me not-even-subtle propaganda whilst also populating itself entirely with unwatchable dross, including run-of-the-mill 'quotes from old people that will blow your MIND!' clickbait bullshit, and the overwhelming majority of the time they just boil down to 'be cool and don't be a dick,' with varying degrees of pomp and pretension, typically on the heavier handed side of ham-fisted, vomit-inducing tripe that makes me wonder what kind of person even feels the need to bother to watch this stuff to the degree that they can bother to sell it so enthusiastically. Bonus chunks get coughed up when the background music is one of *those* songs. You already thought of the tune when I put *those* in italics. If you didn't, you're probably living a better life than most of us.

(8.) *Hitotsu: Izure no Michi nimo Wakare o kanashima-zu*

Izure translates directly as 'sooner or later,' *Michi* once again meaning 'path' or 'road,' in the context of the path one walks. *Nimo* appears to mainly mean 'although,' or 'despite.' *Wakaré* means 'parting' or 'farewell,' but my dictionary only has one of the Kanji lining up with the transliteration, but once again, 400 years of language evolving makes a hell of a difference, even when most of it was spent isolated from the rest of the world. At least, it had better, because I'm banking at least 75% of the differences in my translation being explainable by it. This explanation comes in handy when *Kanashima*, though meaning 'sorrow' and its surrounding contexts such as becoming sorrow or feeling sorrowful, is written differently than in this dictionary. It's like if I wrote the English word *inflamed* as *in-flame-ed*, most of these differences. Regardless, *kanashima-zu* basically translates as the encouragement to have an absence of sorrow.

Sooner or later, paths part. Do not be sorrowful.

I trained myself for many years to be as capable of abiding by this as possible, and I'd say I'm about 94%-95% fully self-asserted in the Obelisk Directive. The last ten percent is always a doozy, and don't even get me started about the last five.

Musashi, being in the last week of his life at the time of saying that, was probably encouraging those around him, including Terao who was inscribing it all, to not lament his passing when that time came. It makes sense. I would do the same.

(9.) *Hitotsu: Ji-Ta tomori urami kakotsu Kokoro nashi*

Machida's translation comes to the rescue when he notes that *Ji-Ta* specifically like that means "I, myself, and others." In the digitized transliteration, I see *tomo-ni*, *together* rather than *tomori*, but ten bucks says it carries the same meaning in this context. *Urami* itself is 'grudge,' once again more split-up in its conjugation than what my dictionary would have it as, but I simultaneously figure linguistic evolution, as well as wonder how Terao was at calligraphy and shorthand. I find myself wondering if he was furiously penning things down as fast as possible as Musashi spoke his last, trying to get everything down and consequently resulting in this 'shorthand feel' to the ascribing. These differences come into context again with *kakotsu*, which apparently roughly means 'to accuse, blame, or hate' as well as 'justify' or 'excuse,' and my only hint so far at that is that *káko* refers to 'the past,' though its written differently, and used in the context of putting the past behind oneself. Once again, we see *kokoro nashi*, which encourages the mind to be absent of the sentence's subject.

I and others together, should be absent of grudge and hatred

Given once again the context of a very fresh in the mind *Sakoku*, Musashi probably still felt slightly responsible for Japan's self-imposed time-out, being a warrior-wanderer in life, though also understanding his actions alone, no matter how grand, could not themselves be what caused the closure of Japan (See the third Principle). Thus, a mentality of shared responsibility for the isolation is logical. However, Musashi also must have surely known and understood that he himself only wanted to do what he believed was right, as is generally the case. Emotions and tensions across the country would still have been exceptionally high in the wake of violence's sudden cessation, and there would have been many hatchets not yet buried, and many vows of retribution unfulfilled. There's truly no simple answer for this sort of weapons-grade debacle, and the only answer I can give is to take matters on a case-by-case basis. But that's far easier said than done, especially on a national scale. Sometimes, hatred is earned through capital offenses and abandonment of morality. Sometimes, hatred is folly and an overreaction that makes clear the hater and not the hated is the problem. Sometimes, hatred is paid back to the hateful and that's fine as long as its in equal and justifiable amount. But that simultaneously goes against this very Principle of Musashi, but by the same token, the crimes of the past cannot and should not be simply treated as water under the bridge. How then, to observe and act upon, without straying into madness? How does one balance the will to learn, the refusal to ignorance, and the demands of justice?

(10.) *Hitotsu: Rembo no Michi omoiyoru Kokoro nashi*

I'm pulling my hair out trying to figure out *Rembo* on my own, though Machida says it means 'love,' in a particularly passionate sense. My lack of resources betrays me once again, and I must defer to this. *Michi* of course, still means 'path' or 'way of', and *omoiyoru* seems to be conjugated instead as *omoi (kanji I still can't find in this dictionary) yo*, suggesting (from my limited knowledge) that this is a point of heightened importance regarding a particular emotional context. In Machida's translation, *omoiyoru* is said to mean 'to indulge in,' and once again *Kokoro nashi* is to say that the mind should be absent of the subject of the tenant.

The mind should be absent of indulging in passionate love's path.

It is a fair point. The excess of emotion clouds reason and substitutes logic with irrationality, which can easily lead to your doom, though I find it hard to believe that Musashi would actively encourage its total renouncement. Granted, 'love' is a sundered word to me, meant only as a quintessential 'get out of jail free' card, a half-baked justification for the most toxic behaviors and habits born of such irrationality, that though it may be true that the committer of such great affront and wrongdoing may feel as though they are in possession of love for whom they have wronged so egregiously, it's more in the sense of an athlete loving their trophies, or a scholar loving their publications, and not even in an honorable sense, instead in the way of coveting the prosperity they have brought. Such empty and soulless love is the pinnacle of the logic of a parent, particularly mothers. Or at least, the one I was unfortunate enough to get stuck with. There's a reason I changed my name, let's just say that.

The reason, by the way, was in large part due to the sheer shame I felt having the same last name as someone so devoid of honor, and so absent respect for my autonomy. That woman has no business practicing medicine as an osteopathic doctor if the twenty-five and a half years I spent sentenced to her shadow made me so sick of life. Every time I have truly wanted to end my own life, the most compelling reason of all was "I wouldn't have to deal with *her* anymore."

Hence, experiencing the phenomenon of love in excess should be avoided, if only because it may prevent you from having such a vengeful and bitter offspring as me. But mark my words, I will have my vengeance for the years I lost, and the years I will lose just trying to claw my way into having years at all.

(11.) *Hitotsu: Mono goto ni Suki konomu Koto nashi*

Mono directly translates as 'thing' or 'object,' so it's a welcome break from the last one causing me such a headache. *Goto* translates as 'everything,' when following a subject, that being *Mono*. Thus, *mono-goto* would mean 'Everything, all of the things.' *Ni* being 'at/on/in,' *Suki* appears to be conjugated as *zu-ki*, but I'm assuming that particular Kanji is *ki* because I really don't feel like checking into public wi-fi to try to scrawl it into google translate to see which particular one it is. In the modern context of my dictionary, *suki* is an adjectival noun used to describe both the people who like, and/or things that are liked. Essentially, it denotes being fond of something. Makes sense. However, historically, as Machida's translation states, *Suki* means "elegance, aesthetics, sophisticated taste." That makes sense too, honestly. *Konómu* is a verb that is 'to like' a particular thing. Once more, *Koto nashi* entails that the mind should be absent of whatever this particular principle is referring to.

The liking of grand elegance and sophistication in all things should be avoided.

I get the feeling Musashi is casting a weapons-grade side-eye at the trend of seeking grand aesthetic beauty in all things, which seemed to be happening at the time (and is honestly repeating itself here in the Pacific Northwest, if you ask me.) In a sense, Musashi is encouraging us to not be that guy at the art gallery who spends eighty minutes staring at a pointillist painting (or any piece in said gallery, for that matter) and going full English teacher 'the curtains are blue because—' at it. I must agree with Musashi on this sentiment. Though appreciation for efficiency and simplicity should be observed, its excess will inevitably find one losing the damn point, and vanishing into a veritable singularity of pretension. Musashi encourages us to not give ourselves prostate orgasms with how far our heads are up our own asses. Musashi would've *hated* Portland with a burning passion rivaled only by my own disdain for the Pretension Singularity whose black hole of ridiculousness threatens to engulf the entire west coast of the US. Jævle.

(12.) *Hitotsu: Shitaku nioite nozomu Kokoro nashi*

    Oh boy, it's another *kokoro nashi* principle. *Shitaku* means 'preparations' or 'arrangements,' but knowing Musashi as a strategist, likely 'preparation'. But it looks nothing like *shitaku* as it appears in my dictionary, nor does it look like *shitaku* as in 'house' or 'private residence', as Machida's translation claims. However, I do find *taku* in the context of housing, *shataku*, 'company housing,' with the same *taku* character as in the digitization. From this, I infer that *shi* in this case would cause the word to mean 'personal or private' housing, but my dictionary doesn't see it. Then again, this is a Japanese to English dictionary, not vise versa, so I can't try to reverse-engineer it that way. But I digress. *Shitaku.* Personal house. The closest thing in my dictionary to *nioite* is *ni ōjite*, which is pretty similar in appearance of writing, which means 'according to,' or 'in accordance with.' *Nioite* does also appear in a previous tenant (6), as a reference to the prior word. Looking at my prior analysis of *nioite*, I'll try to remember to edit my notes on the 6th principle a bit later. Or not. We'll see if I can remember. *Nozomu* translates as 'wish' or 'desire,' but its only written partially akin to how it appears in my dictionary. Linguistic evolution again, I'm betting.

    I'm really not sure how Machida arrives at the conclusion of the Principle being *I will have no luxury within my house,* mainly considering how luxury itself is really not referenced within the wording itself. Unless there's a historical connotation of *nozomu* meaning 'luxuries' or similar, it seems like a bit of an extreme to reach out to, where the word for luxury itself is *zeitaku,* but once again, that's modern Japanese, so grain of salt there. I still also find myself unable to shake off the fact that *shitaku,* by all accounts that I can find, means 'preparation' and not 'private residence'

    If we are to take the meaning of *shitaku* to be 'private residence,' the best I can figure is *Within the home, desire should be absent,* which seems kind of vague and redundant, so I can't really find myself sticking to that. Another possible interpretation is *I will not desire a Private Home,* with the emphasis on the 'private' part to indicate something more like a personal mansion. In this case, that makes some sense. Musashi would indeed frown upon excessively large and fancy homes belonging to a single person and no one else being permitted to use its facilities, as do I. Fake-ass christians and catholics opening megachurches when Jesus would've actually been opening mega-homeless shelters...

    My disdain for religion aside, the alternative interpretation is based on the idea that in this case, *shitaku* does indeed mean 'preparation,' we can arrive at the translations of either *no desire in preparation,* or *I will not wish for preparation.* I wonder if these might have different historical contexts, as they sound more like vague proverbs than anything else. This could mean a terrifyingly large number of different things, but such is the nature of proverbs. In the context of Musashi, I would surmise this to be akin to saying "Never wish for your preparations to become true," i.e., that though a wise king never seeks out war, he must always be prepared for it.

 I honestly find this interpretation far more sensible, considering Musashi. One should not build a nuclear bunker out of hope that the bombs will drop.

I will not wish for my Preparations.

 Preparedness is never a bad idea, but one should not prepare out of a desire to see their preparations become reality, but for in case it does. A true martial artist does not train himself for battle because he wishes to see it happen, but instead because he understands that it very well may happen, and that when it should, he will *not* be on the losing side, and glorious victory shall be attained. Yes, it is entirely possible to both consider victory in battle glorious, whilst adhering to this principle of not actively wishing for it. A very 'with the flow' type attitude towards things, that sees success/victory as glory attained, though also understanding that to wish or seek it in excess is to invite corruption of conscience.

(13.) *Hitotsu: Mi Hitotsu ni Bishoku o konoma-zu*

    Hitotsu in this context is more 'spelled out,' rather than being the single horizontal line to indicate the grammatical organization sense of *hitotsu*, i.e., a new line, conjugated as *hi to tsu*, rather than the former. *Mi* referring to the self, one can infer that *Mi Hitotsu* could be interpreted as 'My lines/my words.' Machida's translation says that using *Hitotsu* in this context emphasizes the previous noun, which would just be to say that 'oneself' should especially take care to keep to this particular Principle closely. *Ni* once again being a noun-following particle for 'at,' 'on,' or 'in.' *Bishoku* on its own doesn't appear in my dictionary, but if I reverse-engineer the conjugation, *bi* translates as 'beauty, while this version of *sho* appears in the context of food (*shokuhin* for 'grocery item,' *shokuji* for 'meal.) Machida's translation has it as 'delicacy/debauchment.' The conjugation of *konomu* and *zu* basically means 'to like not,' which I'm willing to bet is different from 'to not like,' where the former is to be content with the absence of the subject, and the latter is to actively dislike it.

    Myself especially, Delicacy is unneeded.

    Machida's translation has the line as "I will have no delicacies for myself," while also noting that Musashi would not refuse fine food for the sake of others, such as if he were offered it as someone's guest. In peacetime, it was considered a virtue to be partial more to the simple foods that would act as your rations during wartime. However, I'm more than willing to believe that Musashi would find it silly to completely shun the practice of eating well, and not just on the nutrient front, but on taste as well. With careful emphasis on the *delicacy* as the word of choice, Musashi draws a line between just eating well, and eating *finely*. I find it similarly easy to believe that Musashi would frown upon anyone whose diet consisted exclusively of fine-dining level cuisine that *delicacy* specifically would suggest, but also understood that food should taste good sometimes rather than being merely a function of sustenance, damn it. Though it is a virtue, being able to be perfectly content with simple food for the sake of staying alive, it is similarly not something to brag about, that you live oh-so-humbly, and bragging about how you once sustained off of nothing but twigs, leaves, and ants for two weeks somewhat kills the point of being able to. Take pride in your iron gut, sure. But much like bragging of how you retired at twenty-two because you hopped on the cryptocurrency boat early is a surefire way to get shoved off of a mountainside and left for dead, constantly making sure everyone knows how good at survival you are is a surefire way for someone to initiate an impromptu test of your skills.

(14.) *Hitotsu: Suezue Shiromono naru furuki Dôgu Shoji se-zu*

Suezue is an adverb for 'in the (distant) future,' but when paired with *Shiromono* right afterwards it seems to take on the new meaning of "The last generation," though on its own it seems to mean "Substitute," while Machida's translation says it means 'valuable and rare thing' I think we've got another one of those linguistic-evolution buggers again...

All right, so if *naru* essentially means 'to become' or 'to the extent of,' and *furuki* is 'old,' with *Dôgu* being the general word for a tool or implement used to complete a physical task, and *Shoji* meaning 'possession,' with *se-zu* appearing in the context of warning not to engage in whatever subject is being referred to. Now, all I have to do is figure out what sentence this all makes...

In the distant future, artifacts and old tools should not be rare and valued possessions.

I find it not difficult to believe that *furuki-Dôgu* could be taken to mean 'artifact' or 'antiquity,' and I find it similarly easy to believe that Musashi would frown on coveting museum pieces and keeping them for oneself to hoard as valuables, hence the use of the word *possessions* to infer one's *personal* possessions. Though Musashi was going hardcore Buddhist in his twilight years, I find it difficult to believe he was completely against the principle of archiving and preservation of artifacts. A public museum is one thing, but a private collection is another. I'm willing to believe Musashi would support the former, and not the latter, just as I would/do. It is necessary for the continuation of progress, to know what was progressed from, in whatever form that may take. Naturally, one should turn the Vatican into a museum once the catholic church finally falls and christianity becomes as moot as it deserves, i.e., completely. I would rather see tourists taking selfies on the holy see than an old white catholic (or any catholic at all) heading one of the most evil organizations on the planet, if not the single most egregious conclave of evil.

That, or bulldoze the whole damn city and put up a bunch of monoliths saying "This is not a place of honor, no esteemed deed is commemorated here," and the like in as many languages as possible, to warn future generations of the dangers of religions following Mary Sue invisible breathless harbingers of evil masquerading as deities. Any god to be feared is no god at all. It is Demons who demand fear.

(15.) *Hitotsu: Waga-Mi ni itari Monoimi suru Koto nashi*

Waga-mi very clearly is referring to another thing that one should do, considering also we've got another *Koto nashi*-ended Principle, with *Waga* itself being particles denoting and referring to the subject of the sentence, *mi*, or oneself. Machida's translation says *itari* is from the verb *itaru*, 'accomplish,' and I'm gonna have to go with that because my dictionary only has *itaru* in the context of *itaru tokoro*, 'everywhere,' and refuses to elaborate further, let alone on *itaru* itself. I'm willing to bet it makes sense. *Monoimi* also has no clear definition, and everything I can find just points to it meaning 'things,' but that's just *mono* on its own. If the translation as Machida has it, with *Monoimi* meaning 'taboo, moral ban,' then I must be willing to believe that's what it means in its 400-year old context. *Koto nashi* once again tells that the mind should be absent of the subject, with *suru* adding to that point... this one's turning out to be another hard one, considering my relative lack of resources. Let's see what I can piece together...

I should, in my accomplishments, be absent of taboos/superstitions.

This one is kinda kicking my ass a little when it comes to making sense of the script and words and the ordering thereof, but this is certainly a consequence of only having Machida's translation and a modern Japanese-English dictionary to guide me through this endeavor of translating and commentating upon a 400-year old script, whose author and I only relate to each other in our mutual wanderlust, introversion, and fascination with learning and the martial arts.

Machida's translation has this Principle as "I will have trust in myself and never be superstitious," which if that is the true translation, would mean that there's a lot more subtext here than I'm able to glean, but I find it hard to believe that Musashi was particularly vulnerable to Old Man Vagueness Syndrome, or whatever term exists to describe the phenomenon of old wisemen being super vague about absolutely everything. In fact, I find it easy to believe that Musashi, in his youth, may have sworn to himself to *not* be that kind of person in his old age, if he were to make it there.

Regardless, in this Principle, Musashi encourages us to not be superstitious of our accomplishments, and though one should not grow too lax or overconfident as the result of a winning streak, so too should we not grow excessively wary and suspicious of a relative lack of hardship. The phrase 'you never knew you lived on a Death World until you leave' comes to mind. I admit that this conundrum does face me as of late, having escaped Auburn to Port Orchard, though still very much in need to escape America. The band Sugarcult hits a lot differently nowadays, I'll tell you that much.

(16.) *Heigu wa Kakubetsu Yo no Dôgu tashinama-zu*

Though the dictionary I've got doesn't define *Heigu* as 'weapon,' let alone at all for that matter, I have managed to find that it is a specific subset of *Dôgu* essentially meaning 'tools for combat,' which is what Machida's translation has it as. Works for me. *Wa* functions to distinguish the noun as its own thing, acting as a buffer between it and the next word *kakubetsu,* which once again appears nowhere in my dictionary. I curse my lack of resources, that they are relegated exclusively to a modern Japanese-English dictionary which likely lacks many of these words by virtue of them being not as important in modern conversation, and that 400 years is a lot of time for a language to develop and change. I curse also that it is summer, the season of a constant sour mood from me as I was built to deal with cold climates far more so than hot ones, and my patience for bullshit constant pounding heat is effectively zero. I curse also that I'm writing this one stuck in my sardine tin of a tiny house I'm renting because my bike that I normally take to the cafe that I typically work on this volume within needs to go to the shop, and I don't want to risk severe damage on it by riding it when it desperately needs the tune-up. Maybe this wouldn't be such a constant problem if I lived somewhere with less asinine hills. Among my greatest complaints about this miserable state of Washington, alongside how a can of soup costs 3 dollars *if you're lucky*, is that this *is* a place where your route can be uphill both ways, and all that pedaling for the last thirty minutes you just did only got you two miles because the last five were just 'oops, all hills.' I truly hate living here. Maybe it wouldn't be so bad if I were just wandering about and perpetually had enough cash on me to pay for food, drink, and lodging day by day. But no, instead of wandering, I am stuck. This makes Fjellrev a grump fox, rather than a mountain fox.

      Anyways, Machida's translation says that *kakubetsu* means "exceptional, especially important, of the highest grade," so I'll go with it. I've already seen several of these Principles use words and word orders that highlight that 'this Principle is especially important,' which has me slightly annoyed, because if all twenty-two of them are indeed of the highest importance, then none of them are important when compared to each other constantly competing in their wording for highest importance. However, such is the nature of old men to consider what they say to be of the highest importance, constantly. I grow tired of everything being so important. But I digress. Summer is making me incredibly crabby again, as it does. Given that *kakubetsu* is followed by the version of *yo* that ends a sentence as an exclamation, one can infer that *Heigu wa kakubetsu Yo* is akin to saying 'Weapons are very important!' Admittedly, the word ordering within this Principle is very confusing to me, but I'm willing to bet it makes sense as far as 17th century Japanese grammar is concerned, as I understand *no* to be akin to the English apostrophe-s, indicating possession by the preceding noun or clause, while the *yo* character seen is akin to an exclamation point. However, Machida's translation says that *yo* in this case means 'other, the rest, further,' and I'm honestly not entirely sure how.

If the *yo* in this case does mean 'the rest,' then with *tashinama* meaning 'to practice, learn, or have skills,' then with the *-zu* suffix, this Principle confuses me still, especially with the wording that Machida's translation has it as. I don't see any mention within of the self, or of concerns, and yet it says "Weapons are of the highest importance to me, I will not concern myself with other things." Frankly, I'm having a hard time coming to the same conclusion. I arrive at two possibilities:

Weapons are the most important tools, do not stop practicing with them.

My inner nomad resonates with this, in a very 'my sword is my most trusted ally' sense, which also resonates with me. People can randomly turn coat and declare that their allegiance is with evil, rather than honor. Humans can flip-flop their sides like weasels just to better their own situation, rather than take a stand for morality and reason, but the steel at your side will not. When all others are gone, when every hand has turned against you, your weapon will be all the stands with you against the darkness. But this is not a bad thing, for the strength in solitude is that no one can betray you when you're all that's there.

However, I find there is another possible interpretation of this Principle:

Weapons are the most important tools to not have to practice with.

Bruce Lee once said "It is better to be a warrior in a garden, than a gardener in a war," and this interpretation is along with that theme, that the study of weapons and the martial arts is the most important thing that one will hope to never have to use. I hate to beat a dead horse, but Musashi had just seen twelve years of *Sakoku* by the time these words were penned. Whether it caused a crisis of identity, or led to an epiphany, I cannot say. Maybe both took place, the latter after the former as a result of such a drastic change in lifestyle and national focus. When you have studied martial arts for long enough, or at least have developed enough passion for its study, one can't deny that it is a grandly important study indeed. It saves the life of its practitioner when successfully called upon, and may even save the lives of others who were too ignorant to study it themselves, if you're into that sort of thing. These days, I no longer wish to save the world. Maybe a different world, maybe the rest of them, but not this one, and not the Human species. Not anymore.

(17.) *Michi nioite wa Shi o itowa-zu omou*

Michi means 'Path,' and in this case refers to the path of the warrior/path of the sword/the Way, a common theme for Musashi. *Nioite* being 'in accordance with,' and *Shi* in this context is for death or dying. My dictionary is once again stumped on *itowa*, but if it really does mean 'hate, loathe, or deny' as Machida's translation says, then I wonder if it was deliberately left out so that it would be harder to use this dictionary to insult people. How annoying if true, but I digress. It is followed by the *-zu* suffix for a negative, *Omóu* means 'to think/to have the idea of.'

On the Path, death is an undeniable idea.

On the Path and its Ways, death is not a hated thought

The Way is that death is not denied, hated, or loathed, but known.

On this Way, death is undeniable, but not hated.

The first one is a more literal than metaphorical translation, and if we are to dive deeper into it, there are many ways to word this thought that amounts to Musashi reaffirming the most iconic line within the Book of Five Rings, 'the Way of the warrior is resolute acceptance of death.'

There are only so many ways to word this line, that seems to essentially be reiterated here, and allowing us to take solace in that Musashi never strayed from the Way, and always held true to its Path.

Ours is a path of he who stands alone, but this is not a bad thing. There is a difference between being alone, and being lonely. I do not experience the latter, I have trained myself for many years to form and mold The Oldest Truth into my greatest strength. Where many might crumble in aloneness or merely out of fear for it, in solitude there is untold strength, for no one can betray you when you're all that's there. It has been said that to determine the collective intelligence of a team, one needs only to start with a score of a hundred, then deduct ten for each additional person in the team. Too many cooks and all that. Because I turned my lack of allies into my strength, I have little doubt it is why I remain alive today, my ability to not have to rely on others. Unfortunately, however, my training to this end is rather incomplete. It vexes and haunts me, whenever I must ask something of someone else, whenever I might need the aid of another, I try to avoid it, if I can. And in all things, I always hope to avoid needing to involve others. Who knows what chains of obligation they may bind to me and attempt to manipulate my course with, using the weapon of owing favors? Who knows whether or not they even *are* capable of rendering aid? In my experience, it is best not to risk it. Even though I had to be trained in the martial arts by someone, even though I had to learn how to shape wood from someone, I take solace in that they have yet to attempt to cash in those favor chips, as it were. Not to mention that it burns my very soul to have been taught the meaning of honor by someone who has none.

(18.) *Rôshin ni Zaihô Shoryô mochiyuru Kokoro nashi*

Machida has *Rôshin* as 'old person,' while my dictionary says that the word for an old person is *Rōjin* is the word for an old person. Linguistic evolution is fun to sift through, is it not? The *rō* kanji is the same in both, however, and we see the... *mi* character instead of a variant of *shin*? Hang on... well, with the *mi* character itself generally being for idiomatic expressions such as 'one's body' or 'one's person,' akin to how we might say 'time itself' rather than just 'time...' yeah, makes sense. Linguistic evolution is fun to sift through. I cannot find *Zaihô,* or anything close to it in my dictionary that suggests it means 'treasure/wealth' as Machida has it, but I'm willing to bet Machida had a much more complete dictionary than I do. Ironically enough, my dictionary has *Shōryō* as 'a little, a small amount of,' but the kanjis for it are nothing like what's in the digitized transcription. Once again, my lack of resources continues to be my bane. I am similarly willing to chalk it up to linguistic evolution in regards to *mochiyuru* being the word for 'to utilize/exploit,' (exploit in the literal sense, rather than moral) since my more modern dictionary has that as *mochiru*, and is more simply written than it is in the transcription. *Kokoro nashi*, once again, says that this is something one should avoid doing.

The old should not take advantage of treasures and manors.

My reasons are twofold for differing from Machida's translation of 'I will take advantage of no treasure or manor in my old age', the first being that I see no reference to the self in being elderly in the line, with the possible exception of *kokoro nashi*, meaning that the mind should be absent of whatever it is the sentence has described. My other reason is that in the 21st century, the old are insufferable, and fuck them. The gods being the greedy bastards they are take away only those who are fit to stay and make things better, while leaving behind those who should instead be burning in eternal torment. Low and behold, the old seek only to ruin everything for the young, seemingly only out of spite for our very existence, that we do not parrot their thoughts and whims mindlessly. There is no short list of those who I would love nothing more than to break every bone of one at at time, and I am as annoyed with that this fervor is made to exist as I am vengeful for all the wrongs that just won't stop.

(19.) *Busshin wa tôtoshi Busshin o tanoma-zu*

Frankly, I hardly even feel the need to open my dictionary when it comes to *Busshin*. Given that Musashi adopted Buddhism later in life, and it sounds pretty close, I'm willing to bet that *Busshin* means 'Buddha,' or the gods in general, considering this version of the *shin* character, and that Shinto is a thing that exists.

Yeah, I was right. *Busshin* is 'Buddha/the gods,' being a conjugation of *butsu* and *shin*. As for *tôtoshi*, I must again defer to Machida having it as 'holy, venerable, worthy of worship,' as the closest things I can find in my dictionary reference pagoda towers at a place of worship, so it makes sense. *Tanoma* means to request or ask for something/depend on, with the *-zu* suffix being a negative.

Gods are holy, but never rely on them.

I mean, it just sounds like common sense to me. I almost detect quiet resentment in this line, but that just might be my bias against religion, being that the only thing it's good for nowadays is justifying atrocities. Regardless, to rely on the gods is folly, for if relying on them worked, this world wouldn't be such a massive heap of unsalvageable garbage.

(20.) *Mi o sute temo Myôri wa sute-zu*

      Though my dictionary has nothing on *sute* alone, *suteru* means 'to throw away, to discard,' and the Kanji are identical, save for the extra *ru*. Naturally, I'm willing to bet that *sute* on its own is similar, and Machida's translation says that it means to sacrifice or to throw away. Works for me.

      At this point, I've had to return the dictionary to the library, so everything from here on out related to directly translating is largely based on memory, what little knowledge I already possess of the Japanese language, and much more faith in Machida's translation. Granted, Machida's translation has proven most reliable so far, but it is also the case that I have trust issues. Either way, we will forge onward.

      Temo is a term for saying the equivalent of 'even if,' and *Myôri*, in a more modern context, translates as 'fame and profit,' however, in this context, it is associated with honor, specifically the honorable accomplishments and deeds associated with one's name.

      Even though I may sacrifice everything, I will not sacrifice my honor.

      Though Machida's translation has it has '*I will not sacrifice my name,*' one must consider that this Principle seems more to refer to the honor that is associated with oneself or one's name, rather than the raw subject of one's name itself. However, it is also the case that in many circumstances, one's *honor* and one's *name* are pretty much considered one and the same when speaking on such matters. I may be somewhat biased, given that I changed my name in June of 2021, specifically to distance myself from the *dishonor* of the surname that I had, which was shared with two very honorless individuals, one pathologically manipulative, commitment-shirking hyper-entitled egomaniac, and another who unironically believes she can call herself a Gypsy because our family is descendant from Slovak nomads, despite the multiple generations worth of removal and the contemporary interpretation of the word as a slur, rather than a nomadic ethnic group. Her sense of entitlement also seems to promise to outshine our mother's, for all the horror that promises. I've shared joints with people who were on the front lines of Vietnam, only to immediately be on the front lines of Reagan's war on drugs on their return, and they would want *nothing* to do with my wannabe bleeding heart sister. Naturally, my old name was something I was happy to be rid of, and I do find myself biased towards interpreting this line as one's honor rather than strictly one's name. However, I must acknowledge how the two concepts are often interchangeable in many instances.

(21.) *Tsuneni Heihô no Michi o hanare-zu*

With *Tsuneni* meaning 'unfailingly, always, at all times,' and *Heihô* being the word to represent the Path, the Way, the way of the warrior and the learning of martial arts, along with *hanare* being a word for deviation or breaking away from something, this one promises to be the easiest of the lot to translate.

I will never stray from the Path.

This, being the final Principle, would certainly serve to close out Musashi's words with a final affirmation that the Way is something that one should never deviate from, that should always be walked and held true to. With the twenty prior Principles establishing what it means to be a part of the Path, and one who walks it, this final one would indeed close things out with the promise that the twenty prior Principles will always be adhered to, or at least always *should* be adhered to.

And so we now arrive at the final direct-ish translation of the twenty-one Principles of Dokkōdō:

1. Walk the world's Path without dissent to its Ways.
2. I will not plan pleasure.
3. It is extra important to not have a mentality of prejudice.
4. I am an insignificant weight upon the world so grand.

5. Throughout life's passage, do not be dictated by Desire or Greed.
6. My matters are deeds without regret.
7. Good or evil, Jealousy should be absent from one's mind.
8. Sooner or later, paths part. Do not be sorrowful.
9. I and others together should be absent of grudge and hatred.
10. The mind should be absent of indulging in passionate love's path.
11. The liking of grand elegance and sophistication in all things should be avoided.
12. I will not wish for my Preparations.
13. Myself especially, delicacy is unneeded.
14. In the distant future, artifacts and old tools should not be rare and valued possessions.
15. I should, in my accomplishments, be absent of taboo and superstition.
16. Weapons are the most important tools, do not stop practicing with them.
17. On this Path, death is undeniable, but not hated.
18. The old should not take advantage of treasures and manors.
19. Gods are holy, but never rely on them.
20. Even though I may sacrifice everything (else), I will never sacrifice my honor.
21. I will never stray from the Path.

The grain of salt to be taken with this, along with the others that I have been transparent about, is that this is mainly a 'direct' translation, trying to take the words as they are written and put them down in English, in a way that makes sense. However, the literal words placed on paper, and the message they intend to deliver can be two very different things, especially in the case with a language like Japanese.

And so begins the heart of my analysis and commentaries, where I will attempt to interpret these words as close to their Message as possible, and from this, I will write anew the 21 Principles, in a way that may convey their message in the context of 21st century English, as though the man himself lived and died within this era instead, but still possessed all of his experiences, memories, and morals.

1. Walk the World's Path without dissent to its Ways.

When I capitalize words like Path, Ways, and Principles, it is because I internalize them as named concepts. The Path is the name for the lifestyle of the nomadic warrior, an eternal wanderer whose feet may move across continents, but his honor and morality is unbreaking and uncompromising. The Way, conversely, is the ideals of the warrior himself. Granted, in this first principle, the World's Path is not similar to that of the Warrior's Path, but instead in this context means the act of being a wanderer. To walk the path of the world is somewhat literal, walking about in the world, or more accurately, wandering. The Way of the world, however, is one that one wandering warrior is insignificant to. The world will remain the world until the sun expands as a red giant, burning the land and boiling the seas before swallowing it entirely. The lone wanderer does not decide the fate of the world, nor its Path, only that of those upon it, walking their own Paths and going their own Ways. The dissent that one should be without is that of the world's, not its peoples. There is great value in defiance of people walking immoral and corrupt Paths, but this is the Path of people, and not the world.

I will wander the Path of the World, without dissent to its Ways.

2. I will not plan pleasure.

Admittedly, the wording of this Principle is somewhat shallow, though not in the manner of one's self being shallow. More like, it does not convey its message fully. But such is the nature of translating centuries-old text into a modern format, and a language an ocean apart from its native tongue. Naturally, the Message itself is easily lost. However, I may be able to shed some light on this.

One should not plan as though a favorable outcome is guaranteed. To do so is to walk straight into the hands of defeat and perdition. Pleasure itself comes in many forms, whether the catharsis of accomplishment or the prosperity of success, or any other form of thing that makes one feel good. Though it would be similarly folly to plan as though defeat is promised (as this would make one question why even bother to endeavor or plan if loss is guaranteed,) it makes sense to plan for obstacles and roadblocks, and to prepare for a worst-case scenario. The Preparation Paradox is one that can certainly lead to complacency, but mindfulness of it keeps one constantly able to plan.

"I find that plans are useless, but planning is indispensable." —Dwight Eisenhower. To plan for the worst is to assure that one will never be disappointed, and sometimes merely the act of planning for it can ensure that it does not come to pass. Such is the Preparation Paradox, when the act of preparation ensured that the preparations were not needed to be implemented, but this can cause some to wonder what the point of preparing was if it did not need to be implemented. One famously contemporary instance of this was the Y2K bug scare. Hundreds of billions of dollars were spent to avoid the catastrophic implications that were theorized to be ready to tank computers worldwide, and when the new millennium rolled around, the world did not enter a total dark age brought about by global systems going utterly and hopelessly haywire. Many suspect that it was a waste of money as a result, but it is far more likely that because of the spending and the preparations, that is why the Y2K bug essentially didn't happen. Thus, the Preparation Paradox. Musashi tells us to invite it, because it is actually a good thing.

I will not plan as though pleasure is promised.

3. It is extra important to not have a mentality of prejudice.

It somewhat feels as though this Principle is an obvious one, as prejudice is understood in the basic sense to be unhelpful. I cannot really evaluate further on that which is obvious, but I can refine the wording to have a bit more *je ne sais quoi*, as it were.

I will not allow my mind to prejudge against reason.

It is somewhat my intent with this retelling of the 21 Principles, to word them in a manner easily reciteable as an oath to oneself, a promise to act honorably.

4. I am an insignificant weight upon the world so grand.

As I pondered more on this line following my initial translation, I found it relevant in many ways, especially considering the context of this current day and age at time of writing. As corporations and oligarchs plunder and sunder the world and drain it of life, they simultaneously point the finger of blame on the average citizen, who on their own cannot be such a huge sink of resources that it would make a difference in how the planet functions. All of ten corporations produce well over half of the world's waste and pollution, whilst simultaneously telling everyone else that it is the fault of plastic straws and taking long showers, rather than the oil tankers they upend in the ocean. In the words of Yahtzee Croshaw, "I've got three bins and a bicycle I still sometimes use, I'm not the fucking problem!" The efforts of the average citizen are made moot by the greed of the human virus, and Musashi in this line seems to have found something to say that is far more prevalent today than it was in his time. One person can indeed change the course of human history, but one person cannot change the course of the world, for these are two very different things. One person, if they killed a billionaire, would be a hero of the world. One person, by being a billionaire, chokes it with vile zeal and wretched fervor, though it is also the case that there is no functional way for the human race to inflict permanent damage on Earth's biosphere. If the human race all disappeared, the world would return to pre-industrial levels of resources within a few ten million years, and quite honestly, the stars would not miss the evils and vileness of such a horrid species.

I alone cannot be a burden on the world so grand and deep.

5. Throughout life's passage, do not be dictated by Desire or Greed.

It somewhat goes without saying, and yet goes completely without doing as well by the human virus. It seems like basic sense to not let desire and greed be what make your decisions, and yet... the humans continue to prove themselves an inherently evil race, who do not do good out of any innate ability to do so, but to either ward off their evil from completely taking over for another day, or because it *will* benefit them to do so, unless being evil benefits them more. Such are the workings of the human mind, that good is only chosen over evil because they might not get away with it, or because the more directly beneficial choice happens to be the good-moraled one. If a human knows they can get away with evil actions that will benefit them directly, they will overwhelmingly choose this course of action. As said before, the world would not miss their presence if they suddenly were all to vanish. The world would breathe a sigh of relief, and begin to breathe again at last.

What can the final bastions of reason do against such reckless hate? What can those of honor, who must feel like the last of their kind, do in the face of a species that has so thoroughly forsaken it? The only thing left seems to be to stay true to the Path, and stars willing, it will mean some kind of difference, somehow, and that perhaps one day the chance to prove oneself will finally come, but the contempt of the world and its peoples remains absolute, and so it remains so hard to stay decent, when the human virus is the quintessence of evil, willful evil and worship of it, and being the virus is not only encouraged, but rewarded.

I will not be dictated by Desire or Greed.

6. My matters are deeds without regret.

A lack of regret is important for the sanity, but there is a difference between regret and reflection. Where one clings to the actions of the past and disproportionately allows them to influence the present, the other learns from it and allows that influence in controlled amounts, that may change the ending of the story this time, as it were. Knowing the future can change it, and oftentimes, a basic knowledge of history coupled with basic deductive reasoning and pattern recognition skills can feel like knowing the future as decent folk writhe in frustration and fury at the human virus's sheer inability to be decent, to learn from its mistakes, and to even think about improvement.

To be without regret is indeed vital, but there remains the danger of allowing wrongdoing to repeat, and evil to thrive, out of sheer lack of remorse for the sins of one's past actions. How then to balance the drive to improve with the fact that there may very well be a hatchet not yet buried? The hatchet cannot be ignored, lest the blood stained upon it grow more and more enraged at the ignorance of others until it finds hands ready to wield it, unready for the sheer fury it represents, and so history is doomed to be stained in innocent blood forevermore.

The guilty alone must be punished, and if the time is taken to ensure this, that the guilty alone face justice, regret indeed becomes no factor. One must train constantly in discerning between those who must face the hatchet, those who must witness it buried, and those who will place the hatchet into the mound. Or whatever weapon of choice justice is to be delivered by. Regrettably, the gun is simply too imprecise in principle, and takes too little skill to wield correctly, and yet remains so omnipresent *because* of this fact. It is said that 'god did not make man equal, but Samuel Colt did,' this is both for better, and for worse. But how to tell the difference between he who evens the playing field justly, and he who has more power than he should ever have been allowed in a hundred lifetimes?

My deeds will be done without regret.

7. Good or evil, Jealousy should be absent from one's mind.

Many are quick to grouse eternally on how evil jealousy always is. But Musashi here appears to show wisdom well beyond the average human, even more so than usual with this line, with this apparent understanding that jealousy is not always unfounded and unjustified. I personally see Jealousy and Envy as two different things, though many seem to consider them one and the same. Envy is when you covet that which someone else possesses and you do not. Jealousy begins when you wish to deprive the other person of that which you covet, whether taking it for yourself, or destroying it entirely so that none can have it. Perhaps then in this case, Envy is what Musashi warns against, as it is essentially the gateway drug to Jealousy, as it were. Or perhaps not. Musashi seems to understand here, that Jealousy/Envy is not always an unjustified emotion. It is natural to want what you do not have, and natural still to grow envious that someone else may have it. Musashi warns, then, that even though one's Jealousy may be fully rational, it should not be what makes your decision to do act in a particular manner. Decisions may be reached with emotion, but they should not be carried out with it. Emotion begets imprecision, and with this comes error and failure in execution.

Again, I am not saying that emotion should

be purged. What I am saying is that it is valid to allow some level of emotion to weigh in on a decision. But when that choice is made, when the decision must be carried out, emotion must take a back seat to execution, and making sure that whatever it is, it's done right. If Jealousy plagues your decision, it is sure to be absent of correctness. Perhaps when you have made the decision and then proceed to table emotion, logic will then dictate that the decision was wrong, thus allowing the action to be canceled without ruinous consequence.

Whether good or evil in motive, Jealousy will be absent from my Mind.

The difference between the Brain and the Mind is that the Brain is the organ that the Mind resides within, and the Mind is the sum of the Brain's functions and actions, and who you are.

8. Sooner or later, paths part. Do not be sorrowful.

A common line often found in the tenants of wisdom. Perhaps this is because it is sound advice. There are countless ways that this idea has been told across stories, belief systems, films, shows, games, and books. What I find neglecting of many of them is that they always seem to relate to paths parting by way of death. This is not the only way paths part. Sometimes, it is the natural course of time that means that no longer are we in contact with those we once called friends. Sometimes, it is the bitterness of betrayal and the realization that this person is no ally that makes paths part. Sometimes, there is a mutual agreement between parties to go their separate ways. In all of these, Musashi tells us not to be sorrowful that paths part, for that is their Way. What matters is that we remain true to the Path, our own. No true ally would ever demand that you abandon your Path just so that you can join them on theirs.

I will not be sorrowful when paths naturally part.

There is something to be said for the value of defiance, the will to bend your Path that though you remain upon it, you won't have to give up what alliances you have made and wish to keep. Stoicism and resilience are equally valuable, but the Path is a path, not a tunnel. Tunnel vision has no place upon it.

9. I and others together should be absent of grudge and hatred.

It is interesting that Musashi seems to break from his typical pattern of wording to now suddenly say outright that 'others' should do this or that, rather than saying that he or oneself should do this or that, and thus lead by example. Perhaps this is because he placed particular value on the idea of being absent of grudge and hatred. Perhaps it is because I translated the sentence wrong. Perhaps he was trying to speedrun enlightenment and figured that this line, considering the theme of letting go within Buddhism, could earn him extra Enlightenment Points, as it were. Regardless, it is clear that he held to high regard, the principle that grudge and hatred had no place along the Path.

Though I see where he's coming from here, I also find it hard to believe that there should be absolutely no presence of either, lest one become vulnerable to the capital dishonor of willful ignorance. Granted, grudge and hatred on their own carry a connotation of unworthiness in their own rights. Grudges are petty, while Retribution is glorious when done right. Perhaps it is in the execution and justification that separates Grudge from Retribution. Hatred, of course, makes one sloppy in execution. It is often what can lead one to the fallacy of guilty by association, something I do not believe in, and am willing to bet Musashi similarly found to be folly.

It is not easy to do retribution right. But it *can* be done, something that I find is utterly forgotten in this day and age, due in no small part to the constant stream of propaganda from what we otherwise should enjoy as media. Tainted infuriatingly are otherwise excellent shows and films that push a fiction that villains are redeemable. When the protagonist spares the antagonist, it's propaganda. Especially if the protagonist has spent the entire movie making the heads of the antagonist's minions roll. It is not difficult to conclude that this is indeed elitism bleeding into every aspect of media, that tries to purport that the big bad is a redeemable sort, because of course they would say that in hopes that when life imitates art, we will make the mistake of sparing the true criminals of this world, the ones who live in the skyscrapers, that persist in maintaining a system that leaves the streets unjustly vilified.

I will be absent of unworthy hatreds and grudges.

I am willing to believe Musashi also understood the difference between a petty grudge and righteous retribution. It is definitely the case that translating languages leaves absent importances from a message, hence why I am even writing this volume, to fill a gap, a void, left by the absence of the closest thing I can construct to a true message.

10. The mind should be absent of indulging in passionate love's path.

I must agree that this path leads to one going astray. Whether from the Path of the Warrior, from the Path of Reason, or the Path of the Learner, passion threatens rationality. He who wanders alone must not be bound to one place by he or she who stays put. But this presents a most interesting conundrum indeed. What would one do when faced with such a dilemma? When a wanderer meets a settler, and both find themselves truly with feelings for another? I am afraid I cannot properly answer this question, for there is no one in my life who would have such feelings for me that I am aware of, and though I find myself a direct descendant of those who wander rather than those who stay at the fire, I believe I should ponder what I would do in such a strange and surreal situation that I currently consider an impossibility. Nobody in their right mind would feel such a way for a soul as bitter and vengeful as mine, and I even warn others that they should not make friends with me for this fact.

It is a question that has been asked and explored in many films and shows, more contemprarily the most recent (at time of writing) adaptation of Jack Reacher, as well as Into the Badlands: What does a wanderer do, when faced with such passion that they realize, to their horror, that they feel towards another?

Ours is a Path that demands aloneness, for the warrior makes friends and enemies alike in his or her eternal search, their quest for knowledge and improvement of the self. We cannot risk engaging in passionate love, for to have those we care about is to invite our enemies to attack where we are most vulnerable. This is but one threat of many. What would become of us when we lost that which we cared for most? When that enemy does indeed attack at this most vulnerable point, though we may deliver vengeance deserved, though we may teach our foes the true meaning of pain, what becomes of us after? How long will we spend draining pint glasses and bottles alike with regret that we allowed ourselves to make someone else so vulnerable to harm from evildoers by letting them get so close to us?

People like us, we can dream of many ways to make our worst foes feel legendary levels of pain, but I know myself well enough to know that I never want to be so lost in someone else, that these become the only appropriate punishment for someone who would attack me through someone I was foolish enough to care about.

I can only wonder how many would call me cold and callous, but I know myself well enough to know that such an attitude may very well be absolutely necessary, for the protection of my allies. To those who know who they are, I salute you, and apologize.

I will never indulge in an irrational path that will bring me ruin.

11. The liking of grand elegance and sophistication in all things should be avoided.

I feel like this line gets hit the hardest by the fact that translation can leave the Message somewhat lost. These are indeed the words that Musashi said, and that Terao inscribed, but this is far from their Message. Where words are merely what is written on paper or what is typed on a keyboard, the Message is what one should glean from the words. Sometimes they can be one and the same, but when words are separated by centuries and language alike, the Message is all too easily lost.

Musashi seemed to know about 'the curtains are blue' fallacy well before it plagued English teachers the world over. Sometimes a cigar is just a damn cigar, for fuck's sake. I despise the excess of metaphor and symbolism just as much, if not more, and know well that though you may have a shovel, that does not mean you are obligated to dig. Granted, I also acknowledge that there is an anti-intellectualism plague currently sweeping this gods-forsaken purgatory pit of an excuse for a country, but acknowledging that blue curtains may be blue because it's a neat color does not a plague of willful ignorance make.

Of course, this is not limited to symbolism in literature alone, as much as I would love to go on an hours-long rant on why *Gris* and *Sea of Solitude* are objectively bad games that cause the medium to take leaps backwards in legitimacy and value. Grand elegance demands alongside it better craftsmen and more time put into the work, and though there is value and validity beyond doubt in showcase pieces, the two days it took the artisan to make a picture frame could have been spent making a hundred respectable frames instead, to coin a phrase. However, I must emphasize that I am not against putting the extra time and effort into making a masterpiece. Masterpieces, in fact, I believe must exist as exemplars to their crafts, so that all other artisans may look upon it and be able to say 'yes, I will aspire to reach this level of skill, that I may create pieces like this.'

      Regrettably, frustratingly, infuriatingly on levels that cannot be described in any language I know, this seems no longer the effect of a masterpiece, and this is no fault of the artisan who creates them, or the artisan who could be inspired by them. It is the plague that kills creativity perpetuated by the corporations and the leaders thereof who ensure that the walls that divide entry from exclusion are nigh insurmountable. Basic tools cost weeks and months worth of salary. The space to house tools costs more than some will ever know in their lifetimes. Education is for-profit. The will of the artisan's mind is choked like rebar is wrapped around his neck by the fact that capitalism ruins everything, and even the tools they buy break in time to the release of new, more expensive ones. Truly does capitalism ruin everything, for the corpses of men and women who would be the next Einsteins, the next Teslas, the next Musashis, and the next Keatons and Chaplins alike are strewn across the floors of the Amazon warehouse, killed by the earthquake or hurricane that they would have been fired for evacuating from.

I will never demand grandness and elegance in all things.

Let us also reflect and ponder that there is undue pressure on the artisan to create masterpieces from the start, and that the names who were already present unjustly overshadow all others, and the common man asks himself 'why should I support a less experienced artist when I could order from the better one?' The reason is because you must support even the beginners so that they have enough money to become masters. You must support them *because* their name is not worldwide yet, and they need all the help they can get. You must support them, because when the masters you worship retire, die, or become revealed to be repulsive in morals and minds, you will suddenly wonder why there is no one skilled enough to replace them, and you will need only look in a mirror to answer.

12. I will not wish for my Preparations.

I find this line most personally relevant to myself, and that I relate to this line arguably more than any other. Musashi tells us to invite the Preparation Paradox, wherein it is *because* we prepared, our plans became unnecessary. This is a good thing. When it turns out we will not be besieged by our foes, or when it turns out our ride to the tournament or to the pub crawl did not suddenly cancel, we may breathe a sigh of relief that our contingencies were unnecessary. Let us remind ourselves again Eisenhower's words, 'I find that plans are useless, but planning is indispensable.' Let us remind ourselves that Eisenhower also fell for the Red Scare about as hard as McCarthy exploited it, and take his actions with a due grain or pile of salt, but let us also acknowledge that was a damn good line. But I digress.

    One should not build a nuclear bunker out of hope that they will have an excuse to use it. One should not amass weapons and ammunition out of hope they will find themselves in an anarchy that means they may shoot anyone who looks at them funny. One should not prepare a cache of resources out of the hope they will have to distribute them and be seen as a hero for it. We plan because we must, and we ponder because it is right. But the nightmares that we plan to survive, we should not pray for them to come to pass, for nightmares they remain.

    I will not wish for the nightmares I prepare for.

13. Myself especially, delicacy is unneeded.

     Musashi knew well of himself that he did not need 'fine dining' as it were, to satisfy his palate. I know myself well enough to know the same, but I would not refuse an offer of it, mostly out of courtesy to not refuse a fair offer, if nothing else. By all accounts, this was Musashi's attitude as well. Let us ensure that extra attention is paid to the fact that it is not *needed*. I find it hard to believe Musashi was one to utterly deny good food, but easy to believe he did not consider it a high priority. Note that I say 'good' food in the manner of fancy food, as it were, not good food in the way of food that actually works, damn it.

     Musashi could not have possibly predicted the fact that fast food and chain restaurants are as omnipresent as they are in the 21st century. For almost all of human history, it was the case that when you found food, you were to eat it, because there was no telling how long it would be before your next meal. Nowadays, before every highway exit in this purgatory pit of an excuse for a country, a sign reads 'food next right' next to the logos of each restaurant within a mile or two of the exit. If one could compress the entirety of human history into one calendar year, with nowadays being December 31st, the industrial revolution began but two minutes to midnight, the hands that threaten doom.

Regardless, much like the eleventh Principle, this one essentially tells the same message, with the added emphasis that one should not always demand grandness and elegance in what they eat, hence delicacy. However, this is far from advisory to abandon good-tasting food entirely, let alone foods that are especially nutrient-rich and able to keep one's energy up. With the heightened physical activity that martial arts brings in its training when done right comes the need for more food, more often, in order to maintain the training physique and also supply energy to the toughening and growing parts of the body that are being toughened and grown by training. To renounce good food entirely would be madness in the face of this, but Musashi only tells us that we do not need *delicacy*, that we do not *need* those fine-dining foods, but Musashi also quietly acknowledges that if given the chance, there is no need to turn it down. If able, why not? The only conundrum is that in this Grey Century, indulgence to any end is a barrier nigh insurmountable, because capitalism ruins everything.

I will never need luxury and delicacy to bring me satisfaction.

14. In the distant future, artifacts and old tools should not be rare and valued possessions.

There is something to be said about the pursuit of preserving history, and what objects were used to write and make it. To renounce the idea of preservation is to condemn to perdition, but I do not believe Musashi advocated for *that* level of extremity in this line. Rather, that such artifacts and old tools should not be *treasures*, selling for absurd quantities of cash to the highest bidder so that they can lock them away in a private collection that only they and their peers can enjoy. History and its tools should be viewable and learnable from by all, and I'm willing to bet if Musashi lived today, he would be a patron of the Smithsonian Institution, as entry to all of its museums are free of charge, thus ensuring all can view and learn. Education, similarly, should not be a rare and valued possession, simply something that all can undertake and benefit from.

It is also the case I'm willing to bet Musashi believed in not enshrining such relic-level tools, simply because tools are meant to be used, rather than put in a display case and ooh'ed and ahh'ed at by those who have forgotten its purpose. I find myself remembering the *Star Trek* episode *The Sword of Kahless*, where the debate rages on the purpose of the Sword, now that it has been refound after millennia of gathering dust. It is a tool of battle and of hunting, not some dusty relic to be bowed before and worshiped, argues Kor, while Worf affirms that it is not dinnerware to eat skewered game from, and should be treated with the respect that a weapon of such legendary status deserves.

How would one balance the truth of both sides? Both of those sides of the debate are not wrong, but indeed one should not enshrine the Sword and bow before it simply because it is the Sword of Kahless, but indeed it should not be treated as merely another blade in the arsenal, because it is the Sword of Kahless.

This is the purpose that such episodes of *Star Trek* exist for, for us to ask ourselves these questions and ponder them, for they are questions that someone may need to answer one day, and when that day comes, perhaps this episode may be what guides them to do the right thing, whatever that may be. I wonder what Musashi would have thought of that episode. It definitely seems to relate to this Principle.

I will not make treasures of old tools and traditions.

Tradition is just peer pressure from the dead, and though Musashi does not mention the concept of tradition within this Principle, I feel it a necessary add-on in order to deliver the Message of the Principle more effectively.

15. I should, in my accomplishments, be absent of taboo and superstition.

       Here is a Principle that I have been glad to have found lately, as I find myself in dire need to remind myself of it over and over again. Circumstance has not been kind to me over the course of my lifetime, and it is not so much that I am *unlucky* as I am merely *not lucky*. Even then, my unluck remains staggering, comparatively speaking. Those of us who know, know well the feeling of dread that comes with a good streak, wondering when the blindside of rotten luck will hit. The fuckening, thy call it, when that dread is confirmed. 'Ah, there it is, the fuckening' we find ourselves saying when the dark forces of creation rear their ugly head and set their sights on us.

       At time of writing, it is three days until I go to a Karate tournament, and I can certainly feel the crosshairs of circumstance lining up on my back. I find myself asking of myself, how do I balance the need to practice and get tournament-ready whilst also not picking up an injury less than seventy hours before I arrive at the Greater Tacoma Convention and Trade Center for the event? If there is any time this year I injure myself seriously, I cannot help but know in my mind of minds that it will be between now and Saturday, the 24th of September. Beyond this, I still find myself constantly kicking my vigilance into high gear whenever I am without misfortune for seemingly 'too long,' and certainly whenever I encounter good fortune, spending the entire week after in 'Siege Mode,' as it were, waiting for the shoe to drop, waiting for the world to try to kick me off of whatever high horse I have found myself on.

Though I know Musashi would never advocate for complacency, he would have definitely told me to stop meeting every victory of mine with such suspicion, and rightly so. I do my best to not allow my vigilance to keep me away from opportunity, but I cannot deny that my nature of risk-aversion that comes from a youth and adulthood in which I have never been proven wrong to be so vigilant does impact my daily life. Though more oftentimes in good ways rather than bad, I do sometimes face criticism from others for being so constantly ready to go to war.

How to balance the necessity of vigilance with the willingness to take risks and seize opportunity when it presents itself? This is a question that I know I will be facing for many years to come, and I may never have a true answer, even for myself. But in the Grey Century, what else am I to do? I cannot let my guard down lest I risk my absolute annihilation by the hands of a thousand foes, just waiting for their chance to bring me low.

I will not be superstitious of my victories and

accomplishments.

I write this now, after the tournament. I declared it a matter of 'surreal pseudo-victory,' largely knowing that this was a victory by virtue of not being defeat. In two of my divisions, I was the sole competitor. It is admittedly not a large group that is of my age range and rank, because normally, McDojos make black belts of men well before their time to be. I asked myself if I would still have taken first place in those divisions if they were more populated. With one of the scores, I could not say that. With the other, I could. So that was the division I claimed my trophy for. I did decently in sparring.

Overall, I did not slip and fall during my forms, I did not drop my tonfa, I did not get knocked out during sparring, nor was I utterly demolished and earning no points. By virtue of non-defeat, the tournament was a victory to that end. I find myself content with this ruling, so I see no reason to change it.

16. Weapons are the most important tools, do not stop practicing with them.

Like some other Principles, the Message of this one becomes somewhat lost in translation. It comes across initially as something that a dullard edgelord may say, but let me reiterate, this is a consequence of the Message being lost in translation.

When following the Path, and in life in general around humans, the most trustworthy ally you could have is far more often than not, the sword at your side, because cold steel cannot change its mind. It cannot suddenly turn coat and renounce loyalty, having received a better offer for being your enemy instead of friend, as humans are most vulnerable to. Every man has his price, they say. But when your sword stays in hand or at hip, it stays at your side and cannot betray you, this metaphorical loyalty only solidifying itself more and more as the swordsman's skill improves, and as such, his ability to be disarmed is lessened further and further, to his benefit.

Even referring to weapons as the most important 'tools' seems to betray the Message somewhat, but once again, it is often hard to find the word that actually conveys the Message, especially when translating from one language to another. The literal word may not be the correct one, to this end. I can only say this so many times in so many ways. There is a difference between the context of a tool in the hands of a craftsman, and a tool as a thing to be used to achieve an end. In this case, a weapon is the most important tool of the martial artist, and it is even in our title, artist. Much like how a craftsman should never stop practicing his art, so too should a martial artist never stop practicing his. Or hers. Or whatever. You get the idea.

My closest ally is the weapon at my side, and I will never stop training.

This line certainly is a far cry from the translation, but once again, I feel as though this delivers the Message of the Principle more coherently than the literal translation does when put into English. I find myself wondering if my compulsion to reiterate over and over again the loss of Message in translation is a consequence of having to spend my entire life explaining and justifying myself in a dozen ways that I never should've had to, because the social minefield is such that apparently there is no such thing as being able to take words at face value, when I so deliberately choose mine so that one is *supposed* to do that. And so for my bluntness I am condemned to have to constantly explain myself and say more times than I can count that the words I say are the words that I mean, and there isn't some stupid mental gymnastics routine you have to do to figure out what they *mean*, because for fuck's sake, I just *said* what I mean.

Why is simplicity forbidden? Why must it all be so stupidly complicated? Simplicity does not mean unintelligent, just as complexity does not mean sophisticated. In fact, I often find that such complexity is merely frustrating.

The sword at my side will never be so needlessly complex. Sharpened steel is something that requires no such navigation of the social minefield. In fact, in a pinch, it even can assist in that navigation by way of cutting down the less than honorable manipulators and amoral peddlers of supremacism and hatemongering.

17. On this Path, death is undeniable, but not hated.

One of, if not the single most quoted line of Musashi is "The way of the warrior is the resolute acceptance of death." It is often considered the core of Musashi's philosophy regarding the Path, and even in life, that death is so constant and undeniable as a constant, that to despise it would be folly. Musashi understood this well, and it is through this understanding that death comes to all and may do so at its leisure, this awareness of his own mortality, that he lived to die of old age, while meditating in a cave. Caves are cool. I want a cave lair, that'd be awesome. But I digress.

I find myself reminded of the film *The Ballad of Buster Scruggs*, where the title character sees death simply as something that happens to other people, thus his cavalier demeanor in regards to casually inflicting it upon others. For this, he does not survive beyond the first act, brought low by a rider in black far more aware of his own vulnerability. On a rewatch of the scene itself, one might even see a spark of doubt in himself suddenly appear in Scruggs as the black rider addresses him by his proper title, the San Sara Songbird, Herald of Demise. Throughout the preceding story, Scruggs had been perpetually irked by others constantly using just about any other title under the sun, and when this rider in black addresses him as the threat that he is for his skill, Scruggs seems to wonder if this mysterious man is to be his undoing, as he is called by his earned name for seemingly the first time in a very long time, if not the first ever. After fighting countless untrained fools and displaying his marksmanship prowess against the hopelessly unskilled, Scruggs's undoing comes from an equally skilled fighter, who refuses to underestimate his opponent.

    Vigilance is both sword and shield against ignorance, and a trained fighter may be beset constantly by the hopelessly unskilled, whose easy dispatch may indeed make him believe himself invincible, for he may as well be in this case. Musashi never believed himself unbeatable, and one might even argue that his pension for arriving obscenely late to duels in order to frustrate his opponent was based in this fact, and in making sure every possible advantage is on his side, for he knows his own mortality, and that taking advantage of an opponent's impatience is a highly viable tactic, for humans are far more often than not, very impatient creatures.

    I will never deny death its due vigilance.

18. The old should not take advantage of treasures and manors.

There's admittedly not much to say about this one, because it hardly needs elaborating, only implementation. For every time some crotchety old bastard says that youth is wasted on the young, there are countless reasons why fortune is wasted on the old. Musashi was wise in his knowledge that there comes a time when the old must stand aside in order to grant their successors the chance to do better, even if given persons already did well enough. The old, now more than ever, hoard fortune and hide it away from all others with no practical reason, no functional need to do so. There is no reason why their greed should exist, let alone be so frustratingly unchallenged. They stand against those who pose no threat to them, they have no prerogative other than to deprive those that are not themselves. No longer is their goal simply to win, it is to ensure *everyone else loses*. This is their way. It must be brought to end, and if by fire and steel it must be done, then so be it. You will find me on the front lines, fighting in the name of life.

I will not hoard fortune in my old age, when age means I have no use for it.

19. Gods are holy, but never rely on them.

This just seems like common sense to me, as do many of the Principles. My disdain for religion aside, by conventional knowledge, the gods are generally understood to be holy. It is what man does in their name that taints them so, and breeds my contempt for the very idea.

Why rely on what demands you take their word on faith alone? Why ever rely on faith alone? Faith is just a polite way of saying 'fuck it, I'm right,' on any other matter this would be considered selfish, irredeemably egotistical, and utterly shutting out of reason and rationality. But apparently, when you call the divine your justification, the world decides that's just fine?! What kind of blindness is required to believe that this is just?! My only solace is that I find similar contempt in others of my generation, the only thing that gives me hope is that perhaps I am not the only one who can see it this way. But then again, I am always prepared to stand alone. If I must be the last man of honor among a species that has forsaken it, I am not unprepared.

Though the gods may be holy, I will never rely upon them.

20. Even though I may sacrifice everything (else), I will never sacrifice my honor.

One's honor is often associated with their name, and vice versa. It is an odd stance, one that I cannot relate to. I changed my name so that I may begin to put honor to it, without the taint of those who shared my surname at birth. Where one was all to late to begin listening, where one was emotionally abusive and pathologically manipulative, and the other had an adolescence that remains much to be answered for, and nowadays believes themselves entitled to all that they whim, needless to say, a new name was a necessity if I were to begin to create my own identity, and what it means to be me. Perhaps one day, Gregor Fjellrev will have the honor of avenging Greg Laurel's life, the life he should have been permitted to live, instead of one that left him so filled with jaded hatred and dreams of vengeance. Twenty-five years have yet to be answered for, and mark my words, they will be. I may sacrifice everything else in doing this, but I will never give up this name that I have clawed from the grime-infested hands of a surname gone sour, no longer do laurel leaves symbolize victory when those who should represent it are so reprehensible. The only sympathy I feel now is a quiet pity for the person who first chose this name, and that he allowed himself to fall in with such honorless creatures.

Even if I sacrifice all else, I will never sacrifice my honor.

21. I will never stray from the Path.

　　The final Principle, the final affirmation of the oath sworn, to remain true to the Path, and never to falter from it. Though it is clear in his writings that Musashi understood the need to be adaptable, and to be accepting of new knowledge, the Path is not simply a set of rules or a code of ethics. It is a way of life, that allows itself the adaptability to accept new knowledge when it is proven to be truth, and renounce falsehoods when it becomes clear that they are so. However, if you are true to the Path, to the Way of the Warrior, you will find yourself not even needing to renounce falsehoods, because you will have known them from the beginning that they were false. True followers of the Path never doubted for a minute that the thin blue line was a fascist symbol, descendant of slave hunters. True followers of the Path never once fell for the lies of the hatemongering politicians with less brain cells than teeth. True followers of the Path have never allowed their homes or their vehicles to be disgraced with the symbols of hatred, never allowed themselves to fall for their lies, because if you have followed the Path, you will have seen the lies as they are, and you will stand defiant, and you will still stand, because you have trained. To do otherwise is to commit the capital dishonor of submission, of surrender. Forbid defeat, and be Steel and Doom, Skill and Stone. Do not be swayed by those who would infiltrate your sanctums and bring falsehoods to your door. And yet, be prepared to receive new knowledge, though be always skeptical of what does not make sense. Find the answers, walking the Path will guide you to them. It is what I have always done, what I have always aimed to do.

For your consideration, the 21 Principles of Dokkōdō, as written to convey their Message:

I will wander the Path of the World,
without dissent to its ways.
I will not plan as though pleasure is promised.
I will not allow my mind to prejudge against reason.
I alone cannot be a burden
on the world so grand and deep.
I will not be dictated by Desire or Greed.
My deeds will be done without regret.
Whether good or evil in motive,
Jealousy will be absent from my Mind.
I will not be sorrowful when paths naturally part.
I will be absent of unworthy hatreds and grudges.
I will never indulge in an irrational path
that will bring me ruin.
I will never demand grandness
and elegance in all things.
I will not wish for the nightmares I prepare for.
I will never need luxury
and delicacy to bring me satisfaction.
I will not make treasures of old tools and traditions.
I will not be superstitious
of my victories and accomplishments.
My closest ally is the weapon at my side,
and I will never stop training.
I will never deny death its due vigilance.

I will not hoard fortune in my old age,
when age means I have no use for it.
Though the gods may be holy,
I will never rely upon them.
Even if I sacrifice all else,
I will never sacrifice my honor.
I will never stray from the Path.

Sources:

Image: A photograph of the original scripture of the Dokkôdō text as penned by Terao Magonojō

Image: A digitized instance of the text for the purpose of clarity of what is written

"The Last Words of Miyamoto Musashi: An attempt to translate his Dokkôdô;" Bulletin of Nippon Sport Science University, received Oct 31, 2011, Accepted Dec 23, 2011.

Kodashana's Romanized Japanese-English Dictionary, ISBN 4-7700-1603-4

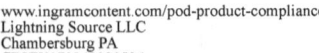
www.ingramcontent.com/pod-product-compliance
Lightning Source LLC
Chambersburg PA
CBHW070240090526

44586CB00035B/1368